Emotions of Me: Maybe of You

HANNIEL KING

Emotions of Me: Maybe of You
Copyright © July 2017 by Hanniel King.
Published in the United States of America by
Gospel 4 U Network

All rights reserved. No part of this book may be reproduced or transmitted in anyway by means, electronic, mechanical, Photocopy, recording or otherwise, without prior permission of the author except as provided by USA copyright law.

Scriptures are taken from the
Holy Bible unless otherwise marked.
ISBN - 978-0-9984665-5-2
Library of Congress Number - 2017946761
Printed in United States of America
July 2017

Content

DEDICATION

FOREWORD

ACKNOWLEDGEMENT

INTRODUCTION

    Fearless 14

    That Parent 17

    She Needs You Too 21

    A Depression 23

    Change 24

    Perception... 27

    Giving Up 30

    A Thought 32

    Normal 33

    Self Love 35

    Lost Ones 37

    Is Freedom Free? 39

    The Way People See Me 41

    When He Left 45

    Knowing 47

More Than You Know	50
Wasted Time	58
Me	60
The Ex Factor	62
The Missing Connection	64
Unfixed	66
Shedding Tears	67
Staying Stupid	69
Leaving Smart	70
I Cried	71
Incomplete	73
A.L.W. Akeem LaLime Wright	74
He Raised His Hands	77
Mr. Man	78
A Response	80
Girl	82
Hurt VS. Forgiveness	84
The Other	88
Harder Stages	90
Stay Gone	93
Love Eludes	95
Something True to Life	98

TO KNK (*My Daughters*)

ABOUT THE AUTHOR

Dedication

To my emotional beauties: Emotions of me –maybe of you is just what it sounds like. This book has been a long time in the making and I have gone through various emotional stages within these pages. The special part about emotions is that they encompass many different reflections and feelings for many people from all walks of life. We may share the same experiences; however the way we channel and reflect on those experiences can be totally different. That is where the maybe part comes in. I love colors so in keeping with the ambitious reds and melancholy blues I present these creative expressions to you. I have compiled these written expressions based on color codes in my life. So, whether you are taking a dip in the red or blue era I am hopeful that you will not only enjoy some of my personal recollections, but just maybe emotions of me will reach out to the emotions in you.

HANNIEL KING

Acknowledgement

First and foremost, I would like to say I love you Lord, this would not be possible without you seeing something in me that the world tried to take back—my life. I give you this heartfelt testimony for without you I am nothing. So here it is:

There is so much to thank you for

I don't even know where to start

You are Alpha and Omega

The mender of broken hearts

When they said that I wouldn't make it

You rescued me and told me I could take it

Even in many last breaths

As I faced death

So sincerely you sent your dove for me

The moment so heavenly as I felt your spirit capture me

The treasure you have given me

No man can measure

In your presence

I feel the ultimate pleasure

I can always be me

Talking with you in the AM

Keeps my spirit free

When my will is not willing

When my body and mind are unstable

You let me know, through you I am able

You are the strongest link in my chain

As the enemy tries to break me

In you I claim the victory

Prayed up in your name I shall remain

I want to thank you for bringing me through every surgery

I want to thank you for allowing life beyond me

Even though the doctor's doubted this possibility

Father God my little girls mean everything to me

I want to thank you for my mother

Words could never express just how much I do love her

I want to thank you for my big sister and every black eye she helped me miss

I want to thank you for my brothers

Tim and Sam, don't ever doubt you are a part of who I am

I want to thank you for my grandmother, Lord you truly favored me when you gave me Valerie

I want to thank you for my father because without him I could never be

Although it takes time to heal the hurts, he is a very special part of me

The list goes on and on

I shall continue to say thank you

Until the day you say, well done Hanniel--- Glad to have you back home.

To Kalliyah

I loved you more than life itself

The moment I saw your face

Not so clear to make out at first

But enough to know that

No one could ever take your place

In my body, we share our space

This I will treasure

You are my lifelong keepsake

Because to me

Your worth more than any breath I take

To think of a day without you is my heartbreak

Mommy loves you

Words could never express

Thank you, God for the gift of my Lee Lee

I am beyond blessed.

To Kayla

Fair skin little nose

10 little fingers, 10 little toes

One of mommy's extra special roses

Almond shaped eyes

Pointy ears

Hair that looks beautiful without care

A smile that lifts the weight of the world of my shoulders

When I hold her

In my body, I helped mold her

You grew beautifully inside me

A bond developed deeply

You are part of the puzzle that completes me

A scent of innocence that captures me

Deep in her body so naturally

I am so happy she came to be

So, glad she was created just for me

I love you beyond expression

I will shower you with my love and affection

Simply is the joy in me for my little girl Kayla.

Foreword

The time is here, the woman, the book! She has so many roles--- mother, friend, daughter, aspiring business woman, great sister, aunt and now author. From the moment, she was born she has been perseverant, classy, humble, and well reserved. Anyone who is a part of her life is blessed. This lady admits she is far from perfect but, she tries to put herself completely into whatever she sets out to do. If anything does not work she lets it go and looks into other possible solutions. In doing this I have seen her accomplish many of her goals. Her commitment speaks through her actions and by the way she carries herself, no one would ever know of her many countless struggles with life and relationships because of her serene spirit and her tenacity to bounce back no matter what may come her way. When she wrote this book, she had her and others in mind. Whoever you are reading this allow yourself the freedom to relate to any era or personal expression that maybe similar to her experiences. I have seen in her God's promise to be faithful and true. It was at two weeks when the adversary tried to take her from this earth. At the risk of losing her, I pleaded with God to let his will be done. Not only did God keep her alive, he also showed off through her. She is a walking testimony of the Lord's many blessings in spite of the challenges that we face in life. She is educated, creative, and hardworking. She has two beautiful daughters that she loves dearly and sets out every day to show them that in this life you can accomplish your dreams. In these expression, you would never have imagined that she would overcome so many storms and face death before even truly living life. She epitomizes the concept of being a true miracle. Through it all she shares a smile, love, and now a book.

-R King
Legal Advocate
Bluzircon and Associates

Introduction

EMOTIONS OF ME: MAYBE OF YOU

A common thread that we share in life is that we all face many different experiences. No matter who you are or who you come in contact with-- you are sure to gain insight into your life and the lives of others. Emotions of Me; Maybe of You are based off my personal experiences. These written expressions hold no direct description of a particular person in my life. Any direct connect is purely coincidental, however these are my personal experiences and perceptions. Take what you can and identify if applicable. If you should happen to discover that you and me share an emotional connection, enjoy the journey.

Peace and Love, Hanniel E. King

*Cover Art Concept and Design by, Kalliyah Wright

PART 1: THE RED ERA

FEARLESS

I don't know myself
I don't know who I am
I can't understand what it is that I am trying to defend
Everything I identified with
I lost in the end
I no longer see a real reason to begin again
I started this journey broken and torn
I push through this journey
Feeling hurt and scorned
Tell me where the lesson is learned
When there is no one to teach
Tell me why you speak so loudly
Yet I can't hear what you preach
From the outside looking in
You would think I have it all
They may never understand that I have nothing at all
The riches I seek to obtain are not merely materialistic

Yes, to the other side I am still just another statistic
Let us pretend that we have missed it
Let us live in lies
To find some sort of alleviation
Let us laugh at all the procrastination
And find joy in rewarding failed expectations
Let us nourish the cap of success and continue to breed lost generations
Oh, wait!
Should I pause? Should I help feed this systematic annihilation?
So am I wrong because I do not want my daughter's knocked up?
Cause it is unlikely that he will want to be cuffed up
So it is okay if you think I am out of touch
Am I wrong because I do not want to see my future sons, my brothers, my sisters locked up?
That makes me too stuck up
So if that is true
I will take the hit
Like marriage, I will say I do
I believe in the power of education

I believe that a people of my pigmentation help to
build this great nation
I believe that we are worth saving
So I will never stop fighting for what is right
I long for the days of true vindication
Man can never understand this
I believe Gods powers are limitless
In this mind frame, I have now become fearless.......

That Parent

That parent I saw waiting in anticipation
Their facial expressions wore the weight of a nation
The sternness was the love talking
Not the frustrations
The look of relief was accepting the fear in every situation
That parent released all control that did not really exist
They understood the value in every last kiss
That parent is not a supermom or super dad
But the love they fight with is limitless
Their defense is impenetrable
They remember this
Cause we can't shield them from the realities of the world
In our eyes they were already our special girl or boy
They had no control of the package they came wrapped in
Yet the world will remind them of the mind and or

body they got trapped in
So who really gets it in the end?
To see them cry
When words are not communicated
And mere verbalizations
Could never reiterate it
Is the reason we hurt on a daily basis
If possible, I would change the world God blessed me to bring you in
To shield you from those times, when your heart will need to mend
What happens when that parent is no longer able to be there?
Who will care like you care?
Who will now wipe their tears?
Who will fight when everyone affirms there is nothing left?
Who will understand how I shaped you until I had nothing left?
I will--- I am
That parent.....

SHE NEEDS YOU TOO

The questions posed
Does the beach need the sand?
They say the boy needs the man
This is something
I want everyone to understand
She also needs you to hold her hand
Watch her take her first steps
Show her it's okay to demand respect
Tell her she does not
Have to settle for neglect
Tell her never settle for less
She is worth more than the very best
Look at her and tell her she's beautiful
She does need you
Let her know the right things to do
Tell her the bad things make you blue
Look at yourself in her eyes
Tell her it's okay to cry
Be there for her first broken heart

From a guy

Tell her it's okay to ask why?

Support her so she can follow her dreams

Mean what you say, say what you mean

She is your little girl

She is a part of you

Just remember she needs a father too...

A DEPRESSION

This real world that I am forced to live in
No time for make pretend
I am forced to adapt my beliefs for survival
Yes I can feel the heat of the invisible rifle
The barrel is pointed at my temple
The Russian and roulette game is no longer simple
This world is murdering my mental
How can people fault others for the skin they are wrapped in?
Did they have a choice?
Do we determine when life should really begin?
If so who makes the right choice?
Who can speak up for the person that has no voice?
I am disgusted by the self-hate that we hold for ourselves
We are all striving in one way or another to make it
There is no mistaking it
I see history repeating itself in approved forms of slavery
Why is it that a person who works a full-time job can't

provide for their family on their salary?
Is this not a sad sight to see?
Why must a person carry a diagnosis just to get help?
Making them feel worthless
Is life not worth it?
We know no human being is perfect
We can laugh and have moments of happiness
Rhetorically --We should be grateful for this
Or is this not a right that we should get to experience?
I don't get it
Can we fix it? Or should we just say nix it
What is going on?
I don't know
It does sadden me to see the way things sometimes go
I don't have all the answers
I don't even have the question
Yes sometimes
Sometimes I am just guessing
Is the whole world stuck in a depression?

CHANGE

Change is inevitable
Hopefully it turns out to be equitable
Because in life there are different levels
Would you be at the top of the hills?
Or are you in the ghettos?
Change- can you see it?
Is it possible for you to be it?
Or are the binders real?
Can only you free it?
The impact can be micro or mezzo
Which factors will determine your level?
Will it be the color of your skin?
The biases you truly hold in the end
The fear in having to begin again
Change- can you see it?
Now think about it
Would it be possible for you to be it?

PERCEPTION

All I can say is you are right about us
All I can do is rely solely on trust
So I can negate the past that hinders both of us
I never try to surpass
The reason behind what I ask
You might think my process is unacceptable
Sorry, but your purpose may not be reputable
Yet you can never begin to understand
What I have been through
Our stories are our stories
To us they ring true
They impact the phases of life we go through
I would say I am sorry
Yes it is true
My apology is to the Lord God almighty, who I owe everything to
He can truly see me
He understands completely

Together in uniformity
Love is given freely
I write this in hopes that you can see
I was not always the person
I have come to be
You would need to understand what it's like to be me
How it feels to give someone your all
With no reciprocity
You would have to empathize with the fact
That my loyalty was not respected
So in some ways you can't relate
To how I was dejected
So---- No I will never again accept it
You would have to know what it's like
Making an ultimate sacrifice
Only to realize nothing would ever suffice
I openly talk to you
You get me
Judgement free
Without having to give the backstory
Is easier for me
Maybe that was not the best way to be

Being with you is done so effortlessly
Would telling you why I am the way that I am
Really make sense in the end
Because you are not him
I am not her
We are not them
Should I just believe that you would treat me the way he did?
Should I concede to the idealized notion?
That I am just another she
Is it wrong to go on what I feel when you are right in front of me?
I understand the reasons for your apprehension
But I prefer to limit my past interactions in all my future decisions…

GIVING UP

I am thinking about throwing the towel in
After all these plays I have no wins
Hate to admit I lost again
The agony of defeat is closing in
No more time for make pretend
Now all my haters can say "I knew it"
People I love question "why I blew it"?
What can I say?
Except y'all--- don't go through it
Yet part of my hurt, they ensue it
So I am thinking about giving up
It shouldn't be so hard considering my luck
This is not me saying I don't care enough
I can acknowledge my mistakes
Okay, your right I messed up
The thing is no one seems to see
All the good that I did
No one shares in the visions that I have for my kids

Everyone is quick to judge me about whom? Why? When? What?

Okay my raters I get it, let's say it together "I messed up"

But never forget I never gave up

When it hit the fan I did more to make up

You crush me so hard

Praying that I break up

I use this to push harder

I thank God almighty that I wake up

People look at me like all I care about is staying caked up

Like a painter's palette

I wear my smile like make up

At the end of the day I still crave a safe touch

When times get tough

When I want to give up

Cause I feel as if I've had enough

It is okay

Keep the cheering section alive anyway

But today won't be the day

Giving up will not be an option that I heed to

That's right I believe I can make it through
So please continue doing what you do
By all means do what's best for you
If giving up is something that I confess
It will be with my very last breath
When my soul is laid down to my eternal rest

A Thought

I am tired of people always having their hand out
Like Comcast they take that on demand route
People always call on Yell
Sometimes they can't seem to understand that I fail
Who helps the helper?
Yell can't even use a hand to complete the count
Of the ones who help her
Honestly this is a sad truth
I have been in this feeling since before my youth
In my childhood, I was ingrained with always help your fellow man
What my mother did not tell me is
Sometimes they really won't give a hand
I speak this with no biases
This hold no respect to a certain person
I can speak this to the ones who shared utero space with me
Cause my mother birthed them

Of this I am certain
I have no obligation to tell you what I am feeling
Yet you have been the very hindrance to my healing
I say this to say
Don't take advantage of the kindness I hold in me
Be my support, stand up, defend me!
Yell--- sweetie your being too friendly
But at the same time
Forgive me
Cause I know all too well that fear of failure
Yes, I know what it feels like to go without shelter
In these moments, it was the fear that failed her
Until you see the beautiful scars that paint her body
And realize that the impossible is possible
It's beyond probable
The miracle of Yell is undeniable
I am not kind because I am foolish
Or easily played
I am kind, because through God I am fearfully and wonderfully made...

NORMAL

Normal, this concept can be harmful
Has the applicability of being different lost its appeal?
Am I wrong for saying what I feel?
Normal definitively encompasses the barriers that placed me in a box
I chose to move forward---never to stop
Change has become looked at as a foreign concept
I guess it would be when looked at through templated context
Ideas of this so called normal I reject
I take time observe, process, and reflect
From my thoughts, I step back
Looking forward to better prospects
It's funny---as a black woman
Are my dreams really limitless?
In my acceptance of Yahuwah in glory
I can picture this
Forget normal
How do you define success?

SELF-LOVE

Self-love is a powerful thing
You should strive to obtain by any means
Even when it seem that you're not worth it
Try to remember you deserve it
To be loved by yourself unconditionally
Never on condition
Leave the conditional love never to be mentioned
Love yourself when you hit rock bottom
And there is no place to go but up
Remember and praise yourself
Because even though you fell down you got up
Leave past mistakes and short comings to the side
Do not I repeat do not allow them to shape the future
Do not allow them to be your guide
If the scar is so deep that even a microscope
Could not find it
Stop looking pretend you have been blinded
If it hurts beyond your physical and mental
Right down to your very soul

If you still have life you still can take control
Many things will seem like it's the end
But it is not over till it's over
You still have time to fight for yourself love and win……

THE LOST ONES

Locked inside a body
Trapped inside a mind
Stuck in an aging desecrating frame
Life and its fragility can never be looked at the same
Empty eyes, smiles without reason
No anticipation for the changing seasons
Rejected, neglected, abused and broken
Not many inquiries for the person
Cursed in utero or maybe just unlucky at birth
Either way it does not matter
No cause or effect takes the latter
When it's the worst, it is the worst
Broken hearts run deep as we search
For a purpose
For understanding
Looking for a higher power
Something/Someone to blame
Where do we begin to feel justification?
Or are we the blame?
Is their fault in the creation of the lost ones?

Words are lost

Found words unspoken

Quality of life changed so we are just left with hoping

Is death really so much worst?

If in this life, you were cursed… to be viewed as a lost one

IS FREEDOM FREE?

Many men, women, and children have paid for
freedom with their lives
A great expense for our countries to continue to thrive
The family that stands by the soldier's grave side
feeling deprived
The crushing pain of a loved one no longer alive
Nations have mourned with deepness of gratitude; with
plaques and memorials and highest honors due
But the reality of the front page news of the diminutive
child accepting their parents Medal of Honor is still
hard to elude.

To think freedom is or will ever be free
Is false sense of security?
All over the world paid in different currency.
If you stop to look closely you will see
Demolished homes of West Bank Village,
When did having a home become a privilege?

Children crying out
Their bellies filled with air
Thirsting so much they drink their tears
Families without a place to call home
I guess there wasn't enough money left after the big bank bail outs to qualify for a loan
We live in a country of choices
So why do we choose so selfishly?
Is it wrong to want a better life for you and me?
The lifestyle so many of us have become accustom to has been fought for
With blood, sweat, tears, man-made deals and world wars
When I hear the word freedom I listen closely
The only thing freedom has that is free are the letters---

F.R.E.E.

The way people see me

Is an illusion
Second by second I have come to that conclusion
They think they know me based on my appearance
Or their perspective comes from a printout reference
Needless to say people are not concerned about my history
The judgment passed down is determined by what they see
I will not blame them for their human nature
I will not even hate them because they are my raters
I will try my best to look beyond what's in front of me
So I can gain an understanding
And process their views accordingly
I'm not going to lie
It impacts me literally
When people judge me on a face sheet
Only to determine my worth by the criteria I meet
As I said I am not going to blame people for their nature

Personally, it just maybe their job to be my rater
If by chance it does not happen to be
Don't judge me solely on what you see
Please get to know the real me!

When He Left

Deeply I am in mourning
Waking up to each new morning
Is hard to comprehend
Day by day, I pray that my heart will mend
My anger that now consumes me
Is because of him
I look in her eyes
My sadness grows
I know I can never fill this hole
Who gave him permission to put a hole in her heart?
She doesn't deserve it
My baby girl I would never expose it
Even though it was him, not you that chose it
I am sorry I could never fix it
No longer could I take the hits, so yes, I called it quits
So, we left quick
This I cannot fix
I have turned cold

I can longer be bold
Once I choose to travel this road
In her I see the good in him
In each in every way from loving him
But I also see the killer within
She could never understand my pain if I am to protect her
I would give her my all
Never to neglect her
I know through Jesus it will get better
Once we make it through the stormy weather
As long as me and Kay are together
For her I just gotta make it
Even if I have to fake it
This heartache I will not let her take it
My baby girl, My world
Also, a void
All because of the innocence he destroyed.

Knowing

Knowing is hard
Living with memories I can't seem to disregard
Stumbling in my moments of pain
Unknown facts
Remain the same
Never speaking holding it in
Realizing one day it will all end
Moving day by day, yet so incredibly stuck
Hoping and praying no one will see your messed up
So many things you would change
If you could go back in time
Just for the guilt you feel to unwind
It is so hard for you to carry
Yet you can't see it's not your responsibility
Living with man-made philosophy
You ask the questions rhetorically
So many lives,
Just this one for you
What should you do?
Knowing finds a way to seep through

To creep into your thoughts
You can't tell anyone
No one would ever see
Just how much knowing hurts me.

More than you know

More than you know I cared
The feelings I shared
More than you know
My heart on my sleeve I did wear
More than you know unclothed and bare
More than you know
Then you could ever see
You never looked beyond the outer
Into a deeper me
More than you know
You took my breath
More than you know I regressed
I know I became a mess
Less and less
I am not feeling so blessed
As I looked in your eyes your truths became my lies
Like those other guys
Decisions I made, not so wise
The Lord says don't have pride

Still I lifted my head and kept my stride
More than you know the deep love I held in me
Just for you so freely.

WASTED TIME

Tell me do you know what it is like to have wasted time?
With someone you thought you would call forever mine
Looking with the blinded eyes of love
Never to see the pattern of the true design
Do you know how it feels to give your all to help another?
Only to find out about the other
Being so selfless to someone
Only to have someone so selfish they can only see their self
Where is the fairness in waiting for them to be in a better situation?
Should you be fair and ignore your feelings?
Wasted time and fleeting moments
Now to the point you wish you could disown it
But have to live with a reminder every waking moment

Where is the atonement?
Not to love you enough beyond their own life's ambitions
Only to learn you are not a part of the greater vision
How can you in any good conscience ever again believe in good intentions?
What happens when nothing can no longer ease the tension?
You realize you have exhausted all possible interventions?
Now let me guess you are expected to play the good role
In spite of no longer being whole
You are supposed to play like everything is on the up and up
When you already know everything is messed up
How in any way can I say?
I put you before me
Yes, it is true that is what I use to do,
I see you would not do the same for me
I know you would do fine if I just wasted some more time

Until you felt like you got what was yours and I got what's mine
Your right the past is the past
But in my future, there is no more room for backlash
Never again will I waste my time
Putting another's wants, needs, and dreams before mine
Because you see nothing is guaranteed
It might turn out they are not what you need
But what about all the in between
I guess that is nothing but wasted time
But who's got time to waste?

ME

There was a time when I could not see you without me
I lived in that sham of a reality
Unfortunately, I was too dumb to see what I had inside of me
I always wanted to please you first
Even though you blindsided me
Even though you never acknowledge what you did to me
Let the past be the past is what you said to me
Somehow you expected us to last
Like you speeding down the highway I was about to crash
So, in hindsight you were right
What is the difference of you seeking me?
But not giving me what I need
I use to hold you to my greed
I no longer do this
When you are gone your softer side is what I missed

Those cold nights when I lay in bed waiting for you kiss
Then something pulls me off cloud nine
And your careless nature with my heart seeps into my mind
Somehow you expected me to maintain my composure and not mind
I thought that honesty would bring you closer to me
Instead you said you feel free like all of a sudden you were indebted to me
I don't think you ever got the point
I wanted you to give of yourself freely
Maybe you feel like you did
I thought we both wanted what was best for our kids
How you can still to this day act like you don't know what you did
I never was the type of woman to doubt herself until I got with you
I always believed in the I do until you made me believe a happily after ever was untrue
I always believed that love would prevail until you convinced me everything is fake

I never believed that wanting to be loved
unconditionally was a mistake
I never believed that giving to others was wrong until
you made me feel it was
I never questioned my knowledge of knowing the
difference between love and like
You always made the wrongs feel so right
I never believed that I was too heavy
Until you said drop fifty pounds then maybe you could
love me
You made me feel like caring wasn't right
Then aha here is the softer side
Bittersweet is the treat
In a way, I'm happy she gets to meet the one I shall
never meet
I have finally admitted my defeat
So maybe she, her, or friend could love you in a way
that I never could
Even though it pains me to say I wish she would
Who you are to her I have never met
Yes, this is one of my many regrets
And who you will be to her I probably won't get to see

Because I'll admit I don't want to see it
After everything I gave from me
But for this resentment
I don't fret
These normal feelings after a loss I accept
I mourn for the loss of what could have been
I hurt for all the years that seem wasted in the end
I mourn for myself of knowing that one day you will realize your full potential and
I won't be by your side reminiscing about all we been through
I mourn because when you touch me I still get weak so from me to you
Silence is what I seek
I mourn for the moment I see you with her thinking in the back of my mind it should have been me
I mourn because I realize I will love you until my very last breath
And I still would give you my everything is what I confess
So, I am grateful for the times you can't bear to ask
I am grateful when you turn me away when I'm mad

EMOTIONS OF ME – MAYBE OF YOU

I am sad; I am hurt
For the strong and unreachable possibilities
The hurt I will feel when you are no longer beside me
I mourn that if my eyes shall close before yours
You still won't see what I fought for
How each day I loved you more and more
How the betrayal hurt me to my very core
How easily you walked out that door like what we had was not worth fighting for
I have hurt others
I have no trust left to give another
So, I miss out on what could be
I am empty of everything beyond just the monetary losses
Admittedly you did not mean to cause this
But everything I held for you inside of me and invested freely
The unreplaceable innocence of what love use to be
I don't know this person that now calls herself ME

PART 2: THE BLUE ERA

THE EX-FACTOR

Something in my past
Took hold of me
Took hold of my path
I could not see my future
So, I did not know it was not meant to last
The ex-factor was always by my side
I never cheated, never lied
Yet this decision alone
The ex-factor would decide
The ex-factor is the one who would wait
Not a drop of my love would he forsake
The feelings of negativity I embraced
So, the heartbreak became mistake
Not a moment of my charity ever faked
I am hurt by the ex-factor
Yes, this emotion is hard for me to capture
Left me in a feeling of rapture
Provided me with a sense of love and protection

Comingled with the gentle sprinkles of rejection
It took me awhile to realize the ex-factor was not the missing connection

THE MISSING CONNECTION

The missing connection
Where do I start?
The man who walked away
Refused to play his part
In my youth, I wondered if he had a heart
I believe he did
I guess it was not strong enough for his forgotten kids
Did he go half on a deed?
To plant some unwanted seeds
Not one though to our wants and our needs
Ran away, like the road runner
I could not catch his speed
So yes, I started feeling mistreated
The hope in me became defeated
The concept of real love I no longer needed
Like MJ doing moon walks--- all he did was beat it
It was so hard to understand why he had to be that type
of man

Why in my hospital bed he was not holding my hand
I guess it was never in his plan
This hurt I bottled up
In those moments, I had to be tough
Cause to me these instances were beyond rough
Mental and physically I had enough
No matter where you lay your head
You're taking the thoughts of us to your bed
Even though you did us rotten
Like my momma said: still we know we were not forgotten
I am not your jury or your judge
I no longer hold a grudge
The issue can be discussed with the almighty
He can hear everything you have to say
Do not worry, the call is not long distance
All you have to do is pray….

Unfixed

Every visit—I listen to the words you speak
My body's so weak
The healing process is incomplete
This feeling I always keep
I can't escape it, I am in too deep
Night after night I toss and turn
As the burning pain of the treatment runs through my arms
I hold in the sound of my cries
Even as I feel the tears fall from my eyes
I have to be strong
I deserve to live, I have to find a way to hold on
My emotions break me down
In this physical ocean, I always drown
I save just enough air to fight another round
Looking on the outside you could never see the broken pieces inside of me----
Literally

Physically I was breaking apart
Mentally I was torn
I am so done being jailed in this bodily form
So, it is okay if I want to quit
Cause truly I know the feeling of being---Unfixed

Shedding Tears

In every letter, I write
I am shedding tears
Not having you here
I am shedding tears
Missing all the fights
Our hard-headed nights
The I wanna be good, but doing wrong always feels so right
Big sister did not know
You helped bring out her inner glow
The place that this world did not get to know
Only with you lil bro did I show
Praying that in this time of difficulty you will grow
Even though you're in lock up
Don't worry, sis got your spot locked up
Because we know more about them pop ups
Instead of helping you they chose the lock up
Sorry that you got cuffed up

If I could I would have traded places
For being homeless should not have been a crime
I understand why you could never take this
This world would get a negative if I could rate this
So together we will face this
It's not easy becoming a man
Double that by the skin your wrapped in
The judge was more than ready to call the end
But please don't ever think the decision was right in the end
So, I'll be shedding tears till I see you again

STAYING STUPID

When I see you
I just want to leave you
Deep in my heart I know I don't need you
I am tired of neglection
Your bold and direct rejection
In my face versions of indiscretion
Staying stupid is being with you
For years I proved this notion to be true
Leave they say—it's easy to do
Guess I failed at that too
The person I know, is not the person I met
Took a gamble
Placed everything on this bet
If I could see pass your face on the first look
Saying hello would not have been a chance I took
The stress and the pressure has got me praying to be free
Before I leave the new you
I must find a way to leave the old me….

LEAVING SMART

Staying stupid
Now leaving smart
Stress free, pressure free
Is what I am now going to be
Sure, I can be replaced
But no one can ever fill my space
Time for me to face reality
Leaving you
Good for you—great for me
It took me a long time to see that I would still be me
Just minus the baggage and loads free
You taught me a lot in the years we shared
Yes, I will admit my judgment was impaired
I did not know how to walk away from neglect
I left myself open for disrespect
These ideas you tried to inject
Mentally I absorbed these lies
I held my head I wiped my eyes
Nonetheless, I am grateful for the time we spent
It is okay if we were not meant

Leaving and moving on
I have finally forgiven myself
No more holding on….

I Cried

I cried- as I sat and ate my food
Not knowing where I would be
Part of me died
Missing you by my side
Feeling my little girl move about
My passing days laced with fear and doubt
I cried
Went up to my room
Drenched in gloom
Wondering if the next time I open my eyes will take place underneath the moon
I hope the stars don't find me too soon
I cried because of the heartbreak
I cried—my soul ached
I cried every tear I had in me,
Until I felt completely empty--- I cried

Incomplete

Completely incomplete is what bothers me
An unguaranteed future is very much realistic
Now I get it
Beauty lies in the eye of the beholder
But what is left when she has no one to hold her
Everybody wants to scold her
Each day the world feels colder
The illusion is time moves slowly
The reality is, time is racing so fast
I love it when it seems like the good times are going to last
My future my past
Which order should those be in?
Would I question the logic in the end?
When I am lying on my death bed
Would I want remember the last words I said?

A.L.W.- Akeem Lalime Wright

A.L.W. how could this be?
How could I have this little one growing inside of me?
I felt scared
For this was something I would hold secret and near
Always I think of you
Dreams continue
Mommy remembers
Your little hands and tiny feet
You came but you weren't complete
Not long enough were your weeks
Doctor's said you were too weak
You were the desire I yearned to keep
No, you were not planned
But you came from a very special man
Precaution were taken to cause a delay
I guess it was not meant to be that way
A.L.W. I regret the many words that I say
It hurts to wonder how we never got the chance to play

It hurts that I never held you
To know that I never smelt the scent of you
To look in your eyes
To tell you how much I love you
To explain why
I cry, remembering the night I said good-bye
Just know with you went a special part of me
To keep you safe along your journey
I love you in each and everyway
In my heart, the memory of you will always stay…

He raised his hand

He raised his hand to beat her
I often wonder how many moments
He took to greet her
When she was away—did he take time to seek her?
He was not her protector, a lax gatekeeper
He was a woman beater
A cold-hearted deceiver
With his all he tried to defeat her
He raised his hand
Tears in my eyes
The deep pain heard in your cries
Echoes of despair in your heart
My love he tore you apart
All because, He raised his hand

MR. MAN

Now let me say this,
You could never take from Peter to pay Paul
Cause you will risk it all despite the fall
Yes, you will put up with the hurt and all
But I know you make the final call
No one could ever disrespect
I know I could still check you
So, recognize what is true
Now anybody can say they can ride
But it takes a special person to know you and stay by your side
And yes, it was me who was there
I'll admit it I still care
I care enough to tell you enough is enough
Even though we have had issues of trust
There is never a moment when I didn't want the best for us
In the moment, another's protection took precedence

over mine
You let me know that we had come to the finish line
See you taught me that in an instant everything could change
You helped me to reject the desire that things would always stay the same
You helped me to believe that nothing lasts forever
Even if the intimate moments don't get no better
Like those wild oceans you were my chosen
But on the flip side you were still searching
You left me hurting
To me you became undeserving
You were never learning
It was like I could cross a million oceans for you
Somehow you would still say my love was untrue
So, I gave you your freedom
No since in staying in the physical sense
When mentally your mind was gone
You were here, but you were not home
See even though you couldn't see how I ride for you
It is okay baby because I would have died for you
I don't worry cause even though you second guess

yourself
I know there's nothing you could not do
If you take your time
Use your mind
To your untapped potential I have never been blind
Please don't play me I know the signs
I always told you I don't share
Just so we are clear once another was able to penetrate your heart
You put everything at stake
On everything I will never be fake
Keeping it 100
Stop making the same mistakes……

A Response

I think of you often

Even when words go unspoken

I remember the wholeness I feel from your embrace

when I am broken

I carry you in my prayers cause you keeping me

hoping

So, until that time we will speak in a language no one

can understand

You need only know that I am by your side holding

your hand

There is no grand plan

There is no scheme of things

I will just be waiting for that moment of honesty

And only you know what that means......

GIRL

I am that girl who has been holding you down
Even when you are not around
I take time to stay positive
I believe in the love we have to give
We only have this one life to live
I do not want to repeat history
But girl, you are leaving me in misery
Is this a conspiracy?
Can't you see how hard it is for me?
I try to show you appreciation
Through detailed dedication
Still you act like this is impossible
You don't want to be responsible
Don't criticize me
Accept me or reject me
Take time to protect me
It's only with you I lay
Remember it is with you I stay
Girl it is for you I do what I do

To yourself always stay true….

Hurt VS. Forgiveness

Hurt verses forgiveness
This feud is endless
Trying to find a way to mend this
Truthfully, I want to end this
In my hurt, I have to forgive
Will it really make it easier for me to live?
If only I could grasp the concept
But this hurt comes in close contact
As I watch as forgiveness falls back
Forgive you
After you hurt me ---you say it so easily
You just can't seem to see
What you have really done to me
Like a joke-hurt laughs at me
While forgiveness watches, so idly
Hurt you have caused tears to run down my face
Forgiveness waits patiently looking for an open space
This feeling I always chase
To break the chains that bind me

All because hurt blinded me
Hurt you are so strong
Forgiveness this is so wrong
I know you two were never meant to get along
Hurt please step aside, so forgiveness can come back home

The Other

He makes me feel wanted just as I am

He never makes me feel like I am less than

He touches me so sensually with his words

That even though we haven't made love yet I can't help but to explode

He makes me feel like I am beautiful

More so than any other

Yes, I believe him when he affirms "I need only you to be my forever"

The way he looks at me is unbelievable

Like he would cross a million oceans to get to my heart

If gaining my love was achievable

His love for me is simply divine

His love was created to be mine

So rare in its purest form

So imperfect, but perfectly perfect for me

I can no longer see clearly where I want to be

Harder Stages

I know you may not understand this

Please don't take this as a diss

I will forever want your kiss

But I am in need of a love that is limitless

I am no longer in need of a man with reservation

Entangled in hesitation

Who gives me a back seat to his relations

I now need more than what ask for

Someone to love, honor, and adore

Of this I no longer question I am sure

I cannot allow myself to be hurt anymore

A lie by omission is a lie nonetheless

Holding onto things that you should confess

Now I am not looking for your replacement

Believe it or not this is a true statement

But my love is going to be earned not taken

Now even though you don't understand what I mean

Remember I was the one

Who gave you everything

I never left your side when you needed me

That part of my love you defeated in me

So sometimes I act carelessly

My own recklessness is detected and myself I have disrespected

My love is not based on whether or not I can mistreat you

It's crazy how I can now raise my hand to beat you

Then I am like damn

Hold up the break through

Somehow those thoughts seep through

I am now someone I don't recognize,

This is nothing new

Its years of hurt, built up frustrations, and lies

There was never a time when I did not see you by my side

Sometimes you were my guide

But you will never be God

But that fight in you inspired me to be better

Like when we making moves together

Cause you make me better

What happens after that's over?

What else matters?

When we are aging and going through life changes

What's left to maintain us?

How can I depend on you when we hit the harder stages?

Stay Gone

When you walk out of my life

Please stay gone

Because if it was not right

Yes, it was wrong

The link has now been broken

I have finally let go

The feeling of hope

I no longer need to show

I will just take this time to grow

Stay gone is what I said

But I prayed you would come back that day

Inside my head—I cursed you

Wished you were dead

But I would have died the moment your blood shed

Stay gone, for the feeling of the unknown

Is a harder reality to accept?

That notion I reject

Don't tell me it will be okay

Don't tell me to be strong

Be on your way, leave me alone

Just do me one favor, stay gone…

Love Eludes

Your love constantly eludes me

I try to catch it but unfortunately

I am never quick enough

Nothing but everything

Seems like a rush

Many nights I dream of your hands touching me

As they tremble so lovingly

As you look into my eyes wanting

And longing only for me

You have no idea of what I desire for us to be

As I think of you

As we welcome a life from each of ours

As we lay under your moon

The browns of my eyes will be your evening stars

My heart for you is always open

Someone that would never take my love for granted

If I stood there with my hand out

He would rather die

Before he would leave me stranded

A heart for a heart as beautiful as mine always deserve a love that surpasses

Realms and ignores time

Are you? Will you? Could you be mine?

If so, where are you?

Can you tell I need you? I grieve for you

Yet that love eludes me

A stabbing and dull cruelty

It haunts me

I see you waiting, longing, and hoping

Yet you never get me

So, I continue waiting, longing, and hoping

Just as I think I am about to reach you the sign says

Sorry this door is no longer open

The owner died from a broken heart waiting, longing, and hoping….

Something true to Life

Sorry I cannot stay

It was my time to go away

I am sorry if I have made you sad

In life, I always tried to make you glad

God called me home that night

I held his hand so tight

I finally decided to let go of my fight

I am in glory now

So please wipe your tears

Collect your frowns

God knew I was in pain

So, he moved some clouds

He held the rain

Although your heart is broke

I hope the memories comfort you

Picture me looking down on you

Smiling at your accomplishments

Inhale me in the fragrance that I sent

Deep down you know this was meant

I will always love you

Even though I am gone

I hope my spirit and my memory will carry you on…

E.L.G

Dear, E.L.G

I miss you so

You were always there to watch me grow

Yes, I was your little mama

Many times, I was the source of your drama

But sharing a part of you was an honor

The hurt you experienced from your father on the chain gang

You expressed, pushed forward, and maintained

Cause a black man in the 30's went by a different name

Sorry they never treated you the same

E.L.G. I hope you remember me

When your spirit is wandering peacefully

EMOTIONS OF ME – MAYBE OF YOU

Shoot a breeze at me

Thank you for those long CHOP visit

Cause I did not have a him

So, for me you did it

I can't even really recall you missing a visit

And that unique knock- oh how I miss it

A slice of pound cake and some Neapolitan ice cream always hit your spot

You could always hold a conversation, sometimes I'd wonder if you would stop

You looked so dapper in your bomber dear jacket

Glad you could have it

The captain of my flight

You helped inspire my fight

So, rest well E.L.G

As always be on the lookout for me

But until then as you said "The struggle continues and the battle goes on. "

TO KNK

My little girls you are my world
Everything I could hope for
God's beauty crafted from the deepest core
There are no words that could express how each day I love you two more
You give me motivation to remember what I strive for
So beautiful are the both of you
The gift of being your mother is truly a blessing
I am so very grateful God assigned the duty to me
I accept the task happily Kalliyah and Kayla you are pieces of life's puzzle that completes me…

Love, Mom

Dedication poem to my two wonderful girls
Kalliyah and Kayla

About The Author

Hanniel King is an active supporter and advocate for people living with physical and mental differences. She believes that changing a life can save a life. Her educational background is in Human Services and Administration. In her free time, she enjoys reading, traveling, and spoken word engagements. Please subscribe to her website for upcoming news and events. She currently resides in in Pennsylvania and is working on two other books. Please visit the website:

https://superdupergirl05.wixsite.com/changealifesavealife

www.ingramcontent.com/pod-product-compliance
Lightning Source LLC
Chambersburg PA
CBHW071149090426
42736CB00012B/2280